English Adventure 6

Student Book

José Luis Morales

Izabella Hearn

English Adventure 6

Pearson Education, 10 Bank Street, White Plains, NY 10606

Staff credits: The people who made up the **English Adventure 6** Student Book team—representing
editorial, production, design, and manufacturing—are Rhea Banker, Elizabeth Carlson, Tracey
Munz Cataldo, Gina DiLillo, Johnnie Farmer, Yoko Mia Hirano, Lucille M. Kennedy, Ed Lamprich,
Linda Moser, Diana Nam, Leslie Patterson, Edith Pullman, Susan Saslow, Leigh Stolle, and Lauren
Weidenman.

Text composition: TSI Graphics

Text font: Gogo VAG Light

Illustrators: Max Calo, Yves Chagnaud, Comicup, Mario Cortes, Valentin Domenech, Marino Gentile,
Philippe Harchy Studio, Alberto de Hoyos, Elisabetta Melaranci, José Luis Pardo, Ferran Rodríguez,
and Roberto Sadí

Photo credits: (l = left, c = center, r = right, t = top, b = bottom) p. 10 (sandwich) Norman Hollands/
Dorling Kindersley, (steak) Renee Comet Photography/StockFood America, (pizza) StockFood
America; p. 14 (t) Bank of China, (cr) Airport Authority Hong Kong, (cl & b) Riksbank; p. 18
(keyboard) CORBIS, (tambourine, guitar, trumpet, drums) Getty Images; p. 20 (cl) Bettmann/
CORBIS, (br) Courtesy of Eman Enterprises/New Miami Studios/Respek Records; p. 26 Library
of Congress, Prints & Photographs Division; p. 28 (AIBO) Sony Corporation; p. 40 (passport)
Erv Schowengerdt; p. 44 (doctor, teacher, firefighter, ballplayer, chef, pilot, actor, famous person,)
CORBIS, (musician) Stock Visuals; p. 48 (cr) Touhig Sion/CORBIS Sygma; p. 68 Foodpix/Sally
Ullman; p. 69 (sandwich) Norman Hollands/Dorling Kindersley, (pizza) StockFood America, (steak)
Renee Comet Photography/StockFood America; p. 70 Getty Images; p. 71 Bettmann/CORBIS; p. 72
Dorling Kindersley; p. 73 © DK Images/British Museum; p. 76 Paul J. Sutton/Duomo/CORBIS; p. 77
(l) Izabella Hearn

ISBN: 0-13-111079-9

Reviewers and Consultants

Adriana González (English Coordinator and Teacher piloting *English Adventure*), IDEO Comunidad
Educativa, Guadalajara, Jalisco; **Sandra Lozano** (English Coordinator and Reviewer), Colegio Matel,
Guadalajara, Jalisco; **Rosa Vázquez** (Principal), **Patricia Hernández** (English Coordinator and
Teacher piloting *English Adventure*), Colegio Medrano, Guadalajara, Jalisco; **Susana Antiga Trujillo**
(Principal and Reviewer), **Janet Quezada Martínez** (Teacher piloting *English Adventure*), Instituto
Guillermo Marconi, Mexico City; **Xóchitl Arvizu, Teresa Contreras, Hilda Martínez** (Reviewers),
Creative Solutions, Mexico City; **Guadalupe Blanco Mata** (English Coordinator and Reviewer), **María
Aurelia García Hernández** (English Teacher piloting *English Adventure*), Escuela Metropolitana La
Luz, Mexico City; **María del Carmen Cano** (Reviewer), Centro de Aprendizaje y Desarrollo Integral,
Mexico City; **Virginia Cerón** (English Coordinator and Teacher piloting *English Adventure*), Colegio
Hernán Cortés, Mexico City; **Rosario Escalada**, Colegio Motolinia, Mexico City; **Ana Claudia
Quintana Lazcano** (Reviewer), Escuela Mexicana Americana, Mexico City; **Guadalupe Torres**
(Reviewer), Colegio Cristóbal Colón, Mexico City; **Yolanda Torres** (English Coordinator and Reviewer),
Salime Piera Castañedo (Teacher piloting *English Adventure*), Agustín García Conde, Mexico City;
Patricia Cantú de Mendoza (Reviewer), Colegio Guadalupe, Nuevo León, Monterrey; **Agustina
Jaime Díaz** (Principal), **San Juana Jaime Luna** (English Coordinator and Teacher piloting *English
Adventure*), Escuela Industria del Vidrio, Nuevo León, Monterrey; **Adelina Ordóñez** (Principal), **Edna
Ramón** (Teacher piloting *English Adventure*), Escuela Antonio L. Rodríguez, Nuevo León, Monterrey;
Liliana Borbolla Romero, Colegio Americano de Cuernavaca, Cuernavaca, Morelos; **Sofía D. Camino
Fernández**, Colegio Miraflores de Cuernavaca, Cuernavaca, Morelos

Printed in the United States of America
1 2 3 4 5 6 7 8 9 10—RRD—09 08 07 06 05

Contents

Character Guide

1 At the Restaurant

The Emperor's New Groove

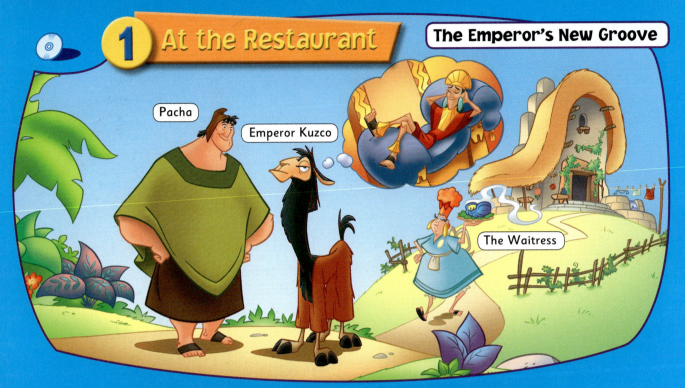

Pacha

Emperor Kuzco

The Waitress

2 They're the Best!

Lilo & Stitch

The Coffee Shop Owner

Nani

The Grand Councilwoman

David

Captain Gantu

Stitch

Lilo

Jumba

3 Inventions

Treasure Planet

John Silver

Jim Hawkins

B.E.N.

4 Experiences

Monsters, Inc.

Sulley

Boo

Celia

Waternoose

Roz

Randall

Mike Wazowski

5 See the World

Pocahontas

- Kocoum
- Powhatan
- Pocahontas
- John Smith
- Grandmother Willow
- Meeko

6 My Dream Job

Mulan

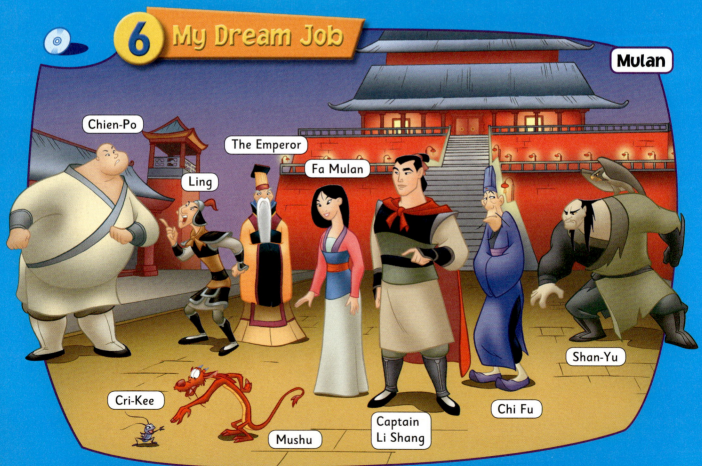

- Chien-Po
- Ling
- The Emperor
- Fa Mulan
- Cri-Kee
- Mushu
- Captain Li Shang
- Chi Fu
- Shan-Yu

7 What Was He Doing?

Aladdin

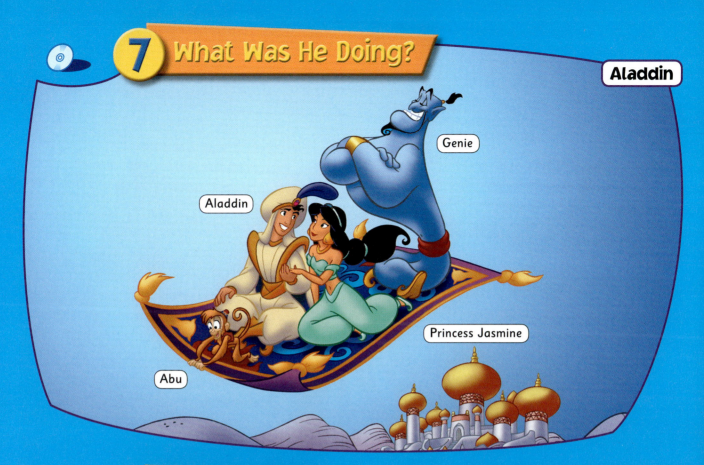

Genie

Aladdin

Princess Jasmine

Abu

8 Party Time

Toy Story 2

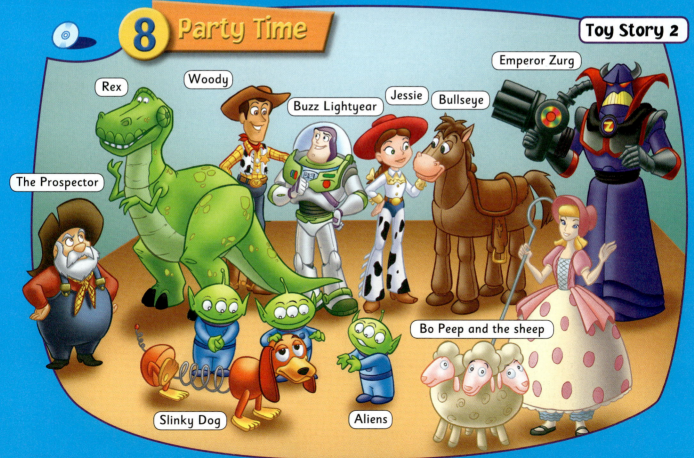

Emperor Zurg

Rex

Woody

Buzz Lightyear

Jessie

Bullseye

The Prospector

Bo Peep and the sheep

Slinky Dog

Aliens

Hello!

1 Listen and say.

So, Mike. Are you looking forward to Sports Day?

Of course! What's your event?

The one hundred meters. What's yours?

I'm doing the 1,500 meters.

Hey, Marina. Do you think you'll win the one hundred meters?

I don't know. I think David's a fast runner. How about you, Coco?

I'm not sure. But I know I'm faster than David!

2 Listen and say. Then listen and number.

a. five hundred
500 ☐

b. one thousand
1,000 ☐

c. fifteen hundred
1,500 ☐

d. ten thousand
10,000 ☐

e. one hundred thousand
100,000 ☐

f. one million
1,000,000 [1]

3 Listen and chant.

I Can Run!

I can run one hundred meters.
I can run one thousand meters.
We can run. We can run.
Run together. Let's have fun!

4  🖊 **Listen and say. Then write.**

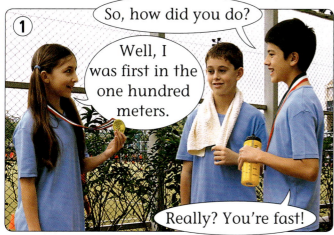

① So, how did you do?

Well, I was first in the one hundred meters.

Really? You're fast!

② How about you, David?

I ran fast. But everyone was faster than me. I was last!

③ I was second!

Well, I was third in the 1,500 meters.

④ You guys are good at running!

But you're the best at baseball!

	Coco	Mike	Marina	David
Event			100 meters	
Position	2nd			

5 💬 🖊 **Ask 3 friends and write.**

Are you good at soccer?

Yes, I am.

1. _____ is good at _____

   _____

2. _____

   _____

3. _____

   _____

9

1 At the Restaurant

1 🔘 **Listen and say.**

What would you like?

Would you like a drink with that?

I'd like a hot dog and fries, please.

Yes, lemonade, please.

2 🔘 **Listen and say. Then listen and number.**

a.  a hamburger ☐

b.  a hot dog ☐

c.  a milkshake ☐

d.  a sandwich ☐

e.  salad ☐

f.  fries ☐

g.  fried chicken ☐

h.  lemonade 1

i.  steak ☐

j.  pizza ☐

3 🔘 💬 **Listen. Then talk together.**

1.

2.

3.

4.

4  **Read and say.**

Explore Grammar

What would	you he she they	like?	I'd We'd He'd She'd They'd	like	a hot dog and fries, please.

Would you like a drink with that?	Yes, lemonade please.	No, thanks.

I'd = I would   We'd = We would   He'd = He would   She'd = She would   They'd = They would

5  **Listen and write.**

1.

I'd like a hamburger and lemonade, please.

2.

3.

4.

6 **Ask and answer.**

What would he like?

He'd like a hamburger and lemonade.

7 🔊 **Listen and say.**

Would you like a hot dog?

It's $2.50.

Sure. How much is it?

8 🔊 **Listen and say. Then listen and number.**

a. 1¢ ☐

b. 25¢ ☐

c. $1 ☐

d. $1.50 ☐

e. $5 ☐

f. $5.27 ☐

g. $10 ☐

9 📙 **Read and say.**

Explore Grammar

| How much is it? | It's $4.50. | How much are they? | They're $8.25. |

10 🎡 **Play.**

Would you like some fries?

Sure. How much are they?

Start

They're $2.50.

Finish

11 **Listen. Then read and write. Role-play.**

1. Pacha and Kuzco are very hungry. They see a restaurant.

Oh no! Look at the sign. Llamas can't eat here.

It's OK. I have an idea.

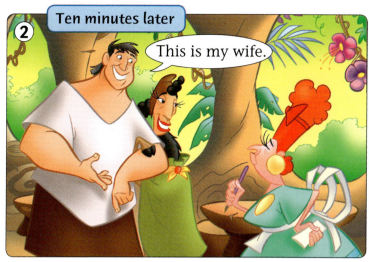

2. Ten minutes later

This is my wife.

3. What would you like?

I'd like the special of the day, please.

I'd like … everything on the menu!

4. The waitress brings the first dish.

It's a bug!

I like bugs. They're delicious!

5. Is everything OK?

I'm not hungry now. The check, please.

6. The waitress brings the check.

Here you are.

How much?

7. I'd like my bug back, please.

1. Can llamas eat at the restaurant? _____

2. What would Kuzco like to eat? _____

_____

Story **13**

Money Around the World

Different countries around the world have different currencies. We found two interesting examples.

Hong Kong

People in Hong Kong use dollars and cents. There are one hundred cents in a dollar. On the 500-dollar bill there's a picture of Hong Kong International Airport. It's one of the busiest airports in Asia—over three million people use it every month!

Hong Kong International Airport

Sweden

People in Sweden use krona and kronor. There are one hundred krona in a kronor. On the 500-kronor bill there's a picture of Karl XI, a king of Sweden in the 17th century. Behind the king is the Riksbank building. It was built in 1668.

The new Riksbank building

13 💬 **Ask and answer.**

1. Do currencies around the world use the same bills?
2. What currency do people use in Hong Kong?
3. How many krona are there in a kronor?
4. What can you see on the 500-kronor bill?

New Words

different, countries, currencies, king, busiest, 17th century, building, was built

14 **Talk about currencies.**

1. What currency do people use in your country?
2. What pictures can you see on the bills of your country?

15 **Write about a currency.**

People in _____ use _____

There are _____

 On the _____ bill, _____

_____

_____

_____

_____

_____

Useful Words

Brazil, Canada, Chile, Colombia, Great Britain, Japan, Peru, the United States, Venezuela

16  **Tell the class.**

Unit Wrap-up

17   **Listen and match. Then write. Chant.** (See page 78.)

a milkshake   salad   a hot dog

steak   pizza   fried chicken

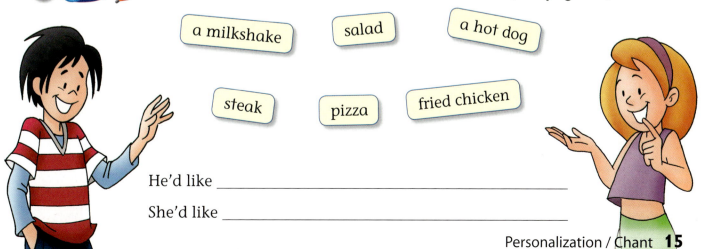

He'd like _____

She'd like _____

2 They're the Best!

1

Listen and say.

(Speech bubbles in photo:)
- Who are you listening to?
- I think the Wonders are better than the Rockets.
- The Rockets. They're really good.
- Yeah, but the Stars are the best!

2 Listen and say. Then listen and match.

a. good **b.** better **c.** the best **d.** bad **e.** worse **f.** the worst

3  Listen. Then talk together.

1.
 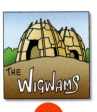

2.
  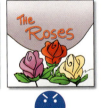

3.

4.

4 🔵 **Listen, say, and write _er_, _more_, _est_, or _most_.**

1.
| cheap | cheap__er__ | the cheap__est__ |

the __most__ expensive | __more__ expensive | expensive

2.
| small | small_____ | the small_____ |

the bigg_____ | bigg_____ | big

3.
| easy | easi_____ | the easi_____ |

Ⓐ Ⓑ Ⓒ

the _____ difficult | _____ difficult | difficult

4.
| quiet | quiet_____ | the quiet_____ |

the loud_____ | loud_____ | loud

5 📙 **Read and say.**

Explore Grammar

| The Rockets CD is | the cheapest. | | Music C is | the most difficult. |

| Which | CD music | is the | cheapest? most difficult? | The Rockets CD Music C | is. |

Which CD's the cheapest? = Which CD is the cheapest?   Music C's the most difficult. = Music C is the most difficult.

6 ✏️ **Write.**

1. (The Rockets CD / cheap) The Rockets CD's the cheapest. _____

2. (Music A / easy) _____

3. (The Stars T-shirt / small) _____

4. (The Minz stereo / loud) _____

7 🔘 **Listen and say.**

Which instrument's the easiest?

The tambourine, I think.

8 🔘 **Listen and say. Then listen and write.**

a. keyboard

b. tambourine

c. guitar

d. trumpet

e. drums

1. most difficult   d
2. easiest
3. loudest
4. quietest
5. most expensive

9 💬 ✏️ **Ask 6 friends and write.**

Which instrument's the most expensive?

The drums, I think.

	Name	Instrument
expensive		
cheap		
difficult		
easy		
loud		
quiet		

10 📖 **Listen. Then read and write. Role-play.**

1 Lilo's sister Nani wanted to find a new job.

I'm looking for a job. Is there one in your coffee shop?

Maybe. Can you make good coffee?

2 Yes, I can. I make the best coffee in Hawaii!

3 Lilo and Stitch waited in the yard.

Here, Stitch. This is a guitar. You play it and it makes music.

4 Stitch played the guitar.

That's very loud, Stitch, but it's good …

5 Stitch tried again. This time the music was louder.

That's better, Stitch. You're really good!

6 Oh, sorry. That's my sister and her dog.

Dog, huh? OK, you both have a job.

Both?

7 One week later …

That's the best guitar-playing dog on the island!

I think it's the only one!

1. What can Nani make? _____

_____

2. Who gets a job at the coffee shop? _____

Listen and read.

The Best Ever!

We asked people to tell us about their favorite book, band, and singer. Here's what they said:

Harry Potter

I think the Harry Potter books are the best. They're easy to read and they're more interesting than other books. Harry Potter is the best!

The Beatles

I think the Beatles are the best band ever! They wrote a lot of famous songs and they're more exciting than today's bands. The Beatles are the best!

Xarah

I think Xarah is the best singer. She's young, but she dances and sings better than a lot of singers who are older than she is. Xarah is the best!

12 💬 **Ask and answer.**

1. Why are Harry Potter books better than other books?
2. What did the Beatles write?
3. Is Xarah old?
4. Why is Xarah better than other singers?

New Words

easy to read, interesting, band, wrote, famous, exciting, singer

13 Talk about music and books.

1. Who is your favorite band or singer? Why?
2. What's your favorite book? Why?

14 Write about your favorite band or book.

My favorite _____

I think _____

_____

_____

_____

_____

_____

_____

_____

15 Tell the class.

Useful Words

beautiful, handsome, popular, shorter, taller

Unit Wrap-up

16 Listen and check. Then write. Sing. (See page 78.)

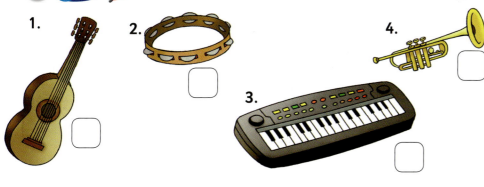

1.   2.   3.   4.   5.

What can they play? _____

_____

Review

1 **Listen and read.**

Kuzco in His Groove!

This is Kuzco. He lived in a beautiful gold palace. It was the most expensive house in the world!

Kuzco liked to dance. He was the best dancer in the world. People didn't stop Kuzco from dancing. If they did, Kuzco got very angry!

Kuzco had one hundred servants in his big palace. When he wanted to eat dinner, he just clapped his hands.

"Oh, Emperor Kuzco. What would you like?" asked the servants. "I'd like the best food in the world!" answered Kuzco.

The chefs made the biggest dinner ever. The food was delicious, but Kuzco still wasn't happy. The servants were scared.

"Would you like anything else?" they asked. "Yes, a knife and fork!" answered Kuzco. It was a bad day for the Emperor!

2 **Ask and answer. Then write.**

1. What did Kuzco like to do? _____

_____

2. What would Kuzco like for dinner? _____

_____

3. Why was Kuzco unhappy? _____

_____

3 🎡 **Play.**

START

1 Who's the best singer ever?

2 What day is it today?

3 Can you play an instrument?

4 **Go back 2 spaces.**

5 What currency do people use in Sweden?

6 Name 5 food items.

7 It's dinner-time! What would you like?

8 What time is it?

9 **Miss a turn!**

10 What did you eat yesterday?

11 Which instrument is the most expensive?

12 **Go forward 2 spaces.**

13 What would you like?

14 Can you swim?

15 How old's your best friend?

16 Name 3 sea animals.

17 **Miss a turn!**

18 When's your birthday?

19 What's the weather like?

20 Do you like surfing?

FINISH

3 Inventions

1 Listen and say.

- What are you doing?
- So when was it invented?
- What was it called?
- I'm reading about the history of the computer.
- It was invented in 1936.
- It was called the Z1.

2 Listen and say. Then listen and write.

a.
seventeen hundred

b.
nineteen fifteen

c.
two thousand six

d.
nineteen ninety-eight

e.
eighteen thirty-nine

f.
one thousand four

1.
1876

2.

3.

4.

3 Listen. Then talk together.

1. jeans
2. TV
3. computer
4. watch

4 📙 Read and say.

Explore Grammar

When	was	the computer	invented?	It	was	invented in	1936.
	were	jeans		They	were		1850.

What	was	it	called?	It	was	called	the Z1.

5 💬 Choose A or B. Then ask and answer.

When was the camera invented?

It was invented in 1900.

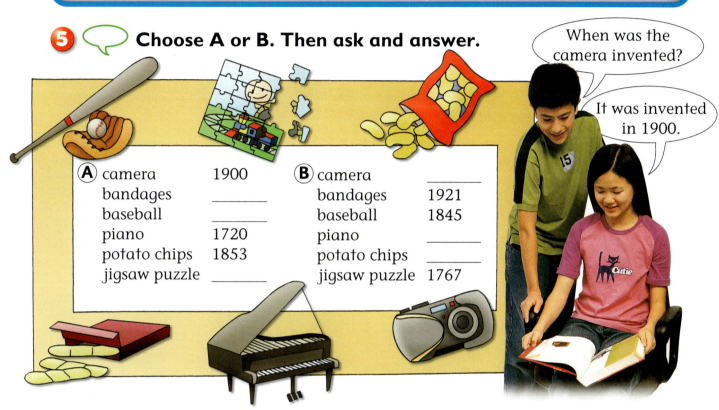

A camera   1900
   bandages   _____
   baseball   _____
   piano   1720
   potato chips   1853
   jigsaw puzzle   _____

B camera   _____
   bandages   1921
   baseball   1845
   piano   _____
   potato chips   _____
   jigsaw puzzle   1767

6 🖊 Write the questions and answers.

1. When were jeans invented?

   They were invented in 1850.

2. When was the piano invented?

   _____

3. _____

   It was invented in 1845.

4. When were potato chips invented?

   _____

Listen, number, and write *ed*, *ew*, or *t*.

studi_____

1 watch _ed_

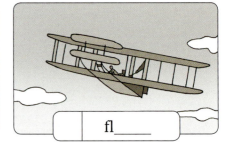
fl_____

fix_____

open_____

buil_____

 Look at 7 and write.

The Wright Brothers

When they were young, the Wright brothers (1) __watched__ birds fly.

They (2)_____ bicycles. In 1892, they (3)_____ a bicycle shop.

In 1899, they (4)_____ flying. They (5)_____ gliders first.

Then in 1903, they (6)_____ the first plane. It was called the Kitty Hawk.

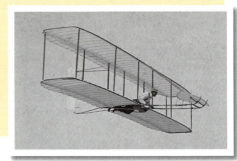

  Write.

1. What did the Wright brothers do in 1892?

   _____

2. What did they do in 1899?

   _____

3. When did they fly the first plane?

   _____

4. What was the plane called?

   _____

10 🔘 ▭ Listen. Then read and write. Role-play.

1 Jim and John Silver went into the treasure room.

Captain Flint's treasure is here!

We're going to be rich!

2

I was here a long time ago … was it 1850 or 2050? I can't remember!

3 There was a dead pirate in the room.

Look! There's Captain Flint. He has something in his hand – it's a part of B.E.N.'s brain!

4 Jim took the robot part.

You were invented with a memory. Why did Flint take it out?

He didn't want me to tell people about the treasure.

5

He didn't want people to steal the treasure.

So what did he do?

He made a trap!

6 Suddenly there was an explosion.

Thanks, B.E.N. Can you remember a little quicker next time?

1. When was B.E.N. in the treasure room? _____

2. Why did Flint take out B.E.N.'s memory? _____

_____

AIBO: The Robot Dog

A robot is a machine that's controlled by a computer. Here's a very special robot dog!

It was invented in 1999 by Sony. It's called AIBO because this means "friend" in Japanese. At first they made only 3,000 dogs. They sold them all in 20 minutes!

AIBO can dance, do tricks, take pictures, and recognize the face and voice of its owner. AIBO's ears even lift up when you talk to it! It can also look happy, sad, angry, and surprised. However, this is not a cheap pet. Each AIBO costs about $2,000!

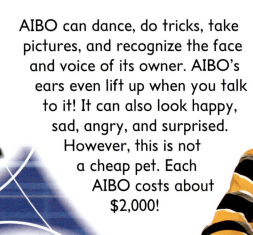

12 💬 **Ask and answer.**

1. When was AIBO invented?
2. What does AIBO mean in Japanese?
3. What can AIBO do?
4. Why can't all children have an AIBO?

New Words

machine, controlled, made, sold, do tricks, recognize, owner, voice, lift up

13 💬 **Talk about robots.**

What kind of robot pet would you like to have? Why?

14 ✏️ **Invent and draw your own robot! Then write.**

MY ROBOT

It was invented _____

It can _____

_____

_____

_____

_____

_____

Useful Words

baby-sit, communicate, imitate, math problems, photography

15 💬 **Tell the class.**

16 💿 ✏️ **Listen and circle the mistakes. Then write. Sing.**
(See page 79.)

1. I studied (geography).

   I studied history.

2. Jeans were invented in 1853.

   _____

   _____

3. It's younger than you and me.

   _____

4. The hot-air balloon was invented in 1763.

   _____

4 Experiences

1 Listen and say.

What are you watching?

I'm watching a show about Italy.

Really? Have you ever been there?

No, I haven't. But I'd like to. Have you?

Yeah, I went there last summer.

2 Listen and say. Then listen and number.

a. play → played → <u>played</u> ☐

b. be → was → <u>been</u> ☐

c. have → had → <u>had</u> ☐

d. practice → practiced → <u>practiced</u> ☐

e. see → saw → <u>seen</u> ☐

f. eat → ate → <u>eaten</u> ☐

g. read → read → <u>read</u> ☐

h. go → went → <u>gone</u> ☐

3 Listen. Then talk together.

1.

be / Colombia ✓

2.

have / headache ✗

3.

practice / judo ✗

4.

eat / pizza ✓

4 📖 Read and say.

Explore Grammar

Have	you they		ever	been	to Europe?	Yes,	I they	have.	No,	I they	haven't.
Has	he she						he she	has.		he she	hasn't.

haven't = have not   hasn't = has not

5 💿 ✏️ Listen and write.

① practiced

judo   tai chi

②

a headache   a cut finger

③

a snake   an elephant

④

pizza   a hamburger

⑤

the piano   baseball

⑥

a newspaper   a comic book

6 💬 Ask and answer.

Have you ever seen an elephant?

No, I haven't.

Yes, I have. OK, my turn. Have you ever played the piano?

Explore Grammar **31**

7 🔊 **Listen and say.**

Have you ever been to the United States?

When did you go?

Where did you go?

Yes, I have.

I went there last year.

I went to New York.

8 ✏️ **Write the questions.**

1. (go) <u>Who did you go with?</u>

   I went to the United States with <u>my sister</u>.

2. (go) _____

   I went there <u>last year</u>.

3. (eat) _____

   I ate <u>hamburgers and hot dogs</u>.

4. (do) _____

   I <u>visited a lot of museums</u>.

9 🎡 **Play.**

START

⚀ Have you ever been to another country?

⚁ Have you ever seen an interesting animal?

⚂ Have you ever eaten any interesting food?

⚃ Have you ever played tennis?

⚄ Have you ever gone camping?

⚅ Have you ever _____ ?

No, I haven't.

Yes, I have.

When ...? What ...? Who ...? Where ...?

10 🔘 📙 **Listen. Then read and write. Role-play.**

1 Mike and Sulley have finished another day at Monsters, Inc.

Have you ever been scared, Sulley?

Uh. No, not really.

2 Never? Have you ever seen anything really horrible?

Nope.

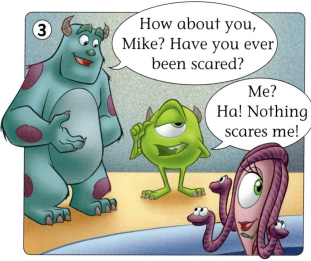

3 How about you, Mike? Have you ever been scared?

Me? Ha! Nothing scares me!

4 Celia sees Mike and smiles.

What about Roz? Are you scared of her?

She doesn't scare me! I'm brave and strong and she's ...

5 Roz suddenly appears.

Wazowski!

Ah! Roz! How ... are ... you?

6 Did you do the paperwork, Wazowski?

Uh ... No ... Ah ... How about tomorrow?

7 Be careful, Wazowski. I'm watching you!

Phew! That was scary!

1. Is Mike scared of Roz? _____

2. What didn't Mike do? _____

Listen and read.

Travel Experiences

There are a lot of interesting countries around the world. Here are some interesting travel experiences:

Have you ever been to Hawaii?

I went to Hawaii last summer with my mom and dad. It was hot and sunny so I needed a lot of sunscreen. I went to the beach and made sandcastles. I went surfing, too. It was really exciting and I had a lot of fun. I want to go again next year!

Have you ever been to Italy?

I went to Italy for my last vacation with my aunt and uncle. We visited Rome and saw a lot of old and famous places, like the Trevi Fountain. We ate pizza but we didn't have lasagna. I wanted to eat lasagna because I haven't eaten it before. Well, maybe next time!

12 💬 **Ask and answer.**

1. What was the weather like in Hawaii?
2. What did David do on the beach?
3. What did Marina do in Rome?
4. Has Marina ever eaten lasagna?

New Words

experiences, sandcastles, slept, Rome, lasagna

13 **Talk about vacations.**

Where did you go for your last vacation? What did you do?

14 **Write about your last vacation.**

My Last Vacation

I went to _____

_____

_____

_____

_____

_____

Useful Words

ate pizza, bought some presents, drank orange juice, met new friends, saw a giraffe, took pictures

15 **Tell the class.**

Unit Wrap-up

16   **Listen and write two items. Then sing.** (See page 79.)

1. She's had

_____ and

_____

2. She's eaten

_____ and

_____

3. She's watched

_____ and

_____

4. She's played

_____ and

_____

Personalization / Song **35**

1   **Listen and read.**

The Best Adventure Ever!

This is the R.L.S. Legacy. The ship was built a long time ago. Jim Hawkins and John Silver took the ship to Treasure Planet.

Life was difficult for Jim on the ship. John Silver gave Jim a lot of jobs. He had to clean the floors and wash the dishes.

Jim didn't like the jobs and he was always tired. But, every time he looked at the stars in space, he was happy again.

"Have you ever been on a boat in space?" asked John Silver. "No, I haven't," answered Jim.

They went to the bottom of the ship together and climbed on the boat. Jim was excited. He always wanted to fly a boat in space!

Jim flew the boat really fast. He turned to John Silver and said, "This is great! It's the best adventure I've ever had!"

2   **Ask and answer. Then write.**

1. What was the ship called? _____

2. What did Jim have to do? _____

_____

3. Where did Jim and John go? _____

_____

3 Play.

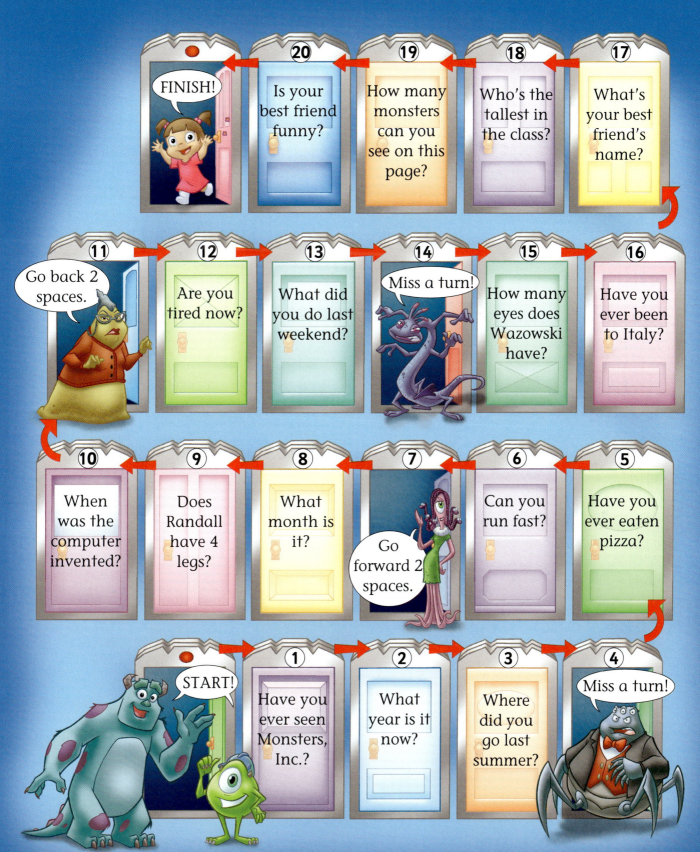

20 Is your best friend funny?

19 How many monsters can you see on this page?

18 Who's the tallest in the class?

17 What's your best friend's name?

FINISH!

11 Go back 2 spaces.

12 Are you tired now?

13 What did you do last weekend?

14 Miss a turn!

15 How many eyes does Wazowski have?

16 Have you ever been to Italy?

10 When was the computer invented?

9 Does Randall have 4 legs?

8 What month is it?

7 Go forward 2 spaces.

6 Can you run fast?

5 Have you ever eaten pizza?

START!

1 Have you ever seen Monsters, Inc.?

2 What year is it now?

3 Where did you go last summer?

4 Miss a turn!

5 See the World

1 Listen and say.

I'm looking forward to our visit to Houston.

What will you do first?

Then you'll need a guidebook.

Yes, it will be fun staying with our host family.

I don't know. Maybe I'll explore the city.

2 Listen and say. Then listen and number in order.

a. make some new friends

b. meet the host family

c. study at a language school

d. explore the city

e. go to the airport

f. fly to Houston

3 Listen. Then talk together.

1. city   2. school   3. host family   4. new friends

4 Read and say.

Explore Grammar

| What will | we
they
he
she | do? | We'll
They'll
He'll
She'll | explore | the city. | We
They
He
She | won't explore | the city. |

I'll = I will   You'll = You will   He'll = He will   She'll = She will   They'll = They will   Won't = Will not

5 Listen and say. Then write.

Houston

1. First, _____

2. Next, _____

3. After that, _____

4. Then, _____

6 Choose A or B. Then ask and answer.

What will you do first?

First, I'll go to the airport at 9 o'clock. Next, …

A
1. Go to airport at 9 o'clock.
2. Fly to Houston.
3. Meet host family.
4. Go shopping in the afternoon.

B
1. Go to host family's home.
2. Have dinner with host family.
3. Explore the city.
4. Go home and go to bed!

7 🔵 ✏️ **Listen and say. Then listen and check. Write.**

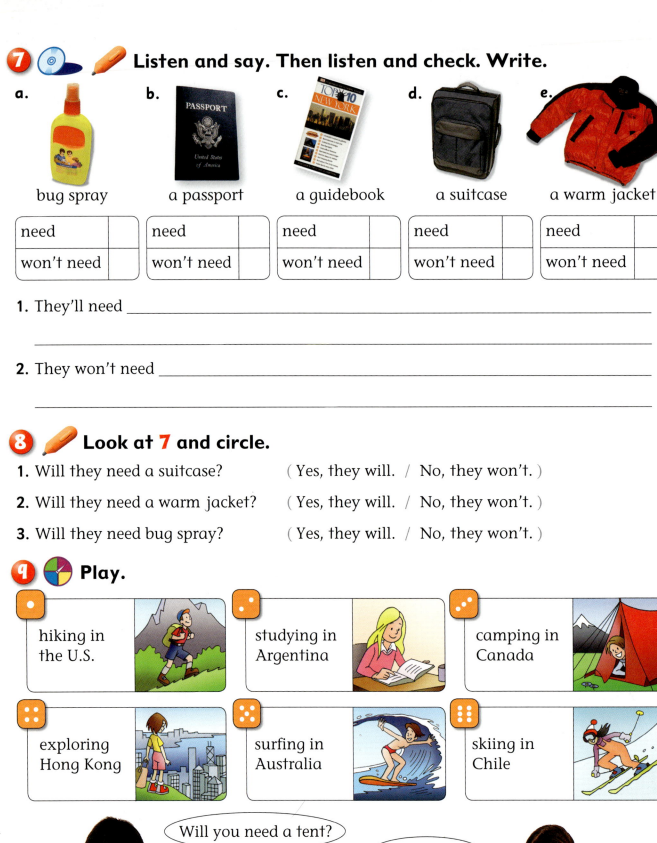

a. bug spray
b. a passport
c. a guidebook
d. a suitcase
e. a warm jacket

need	
won't need	

need	
won't need	

need	
won't need	

need	
won't need	

need	
won't need	

1. They'll need _____

_____

2. They won't need _____

_____

8 ✏️ **Look at 7 and circle.**

1. Will they need a suitcase? (Yes, they will. / No, they won't.)

2. Will they need a warm jacket? (Yes, they will. / No, they won't.)

3. Will they need bug spray? (Yes, they will. / No, they won't.)

9 🎡 **Play.**

⚀ hiking in the U.S.

⚁ studying in Argentina

⚂ camping in Canada

⚃ exploring Hong Kong

⚄ surfing in Australia

⚅ skiing in Chile

Will you need a tent?

No, I won't.

Will you need a warm jacket?

Yes, I will.

Are you going skiing in Chile?

Yes, I am!

10 **Listen. Then read and write. Role-play.**

1 John Smith and Pocahontas are planning a trip to England.

When I get to England, what will I do first?

2 First, I'll take you to my home.

3 Then, we'll go to the palace.

Will I meet the King?

4 Yes, you will.

Oh! Then I'll need a present from my country.

5 Meeko has an idea.

No, it has to be something special.

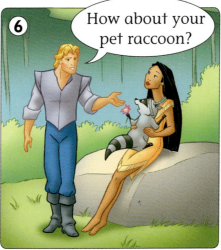

6 How about your pet raccoon?

7 Meeko?

I guess that's a bad idea!

1. Where will Pocahontas go? _____

2. What will Pocahontas need? _____

_____

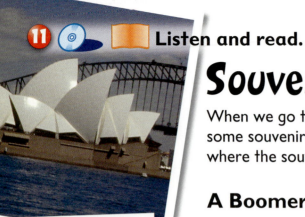

Souvenir Quiz

When we go to another country we often bring back some souvenirs. Below are two examples. Can you guess where the souvenirs are from?

A Boomerang

When you go to this country, you'll see this souvenir. It's called a boomerang. It's made of wood and you can see painted animals on it, such as the kangaroo. A boomerang is a great souvenir for your friends. When you throw it, it will come back to you! Where's this souvenir from?

a. Brazil   **b.** Egypt   **c.** Australia

Maple Syrup

When you go to this country, you'll see this souvenir. It's called maple syrup. It's made from maple trees and it's used on pancakes. Maple syrup is a great souvenir for your family. It tastes really good! Where's this souvenir from?

a. Canada   **b.** France   **c.** Kenya

12 💬 **Ask and answer.**

1. What's a boomerang made of?
2. What happens when you throw a boomerang?
3. What's maple syrup made from?
4. Why is maple syrup a great souvenir?

New Words

quiz, bring back, souvenir, boomerang, made of wood, kangaroo, throw, come back, maple syrup, made from maple trees, used on pancakes, tastes

13 💬 **Talk about souvenirs.**

1. What are some interesting souvenirs from your country?
2. Have you ever bought a souvenir?

14 ✏️ **Write about a souvenir.**

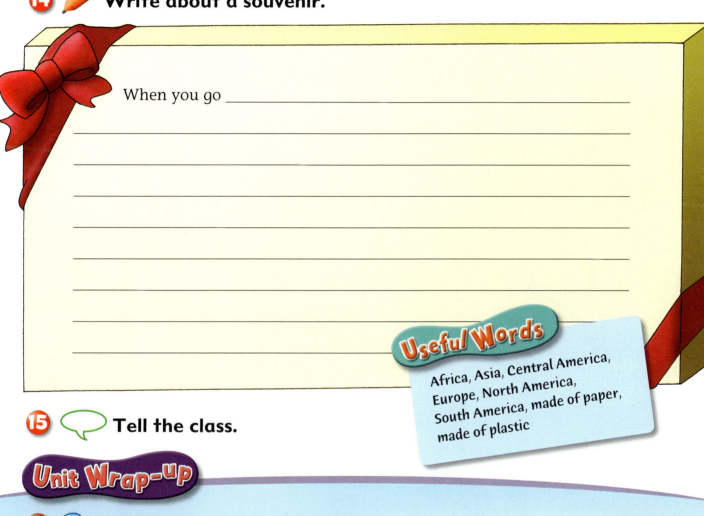

When you go _____

_____

_____

_____

_____

_____

_____

Useful Words

Africa, Asia, Central America, Europe, North America, South America, made of paper, made of plastic

15 💬 **Tell the class.**

Unit Wrap-up

16 💿 **Listen and check. Sing. (See page 79.)**

1. Where will they go? ☐ Italy ☐ Canada

2. What will they study? ☐ English ☐ Italian

3. What will they need in Hong Kong? ☐ a suitcase ☐ money

4. What won't they need? ☐ a warm jacket ☐ a passport

6 My Dream Job

1 🔘 **Listen and say.**

What do you want to be when you're older, David?

Why do you want to be an actor?

I want to be an actor!

Because I want to be rich and famous!

2 🔘 **Listen and say. Then listen and number.**

 a. a doctor ☐

 b. a teacher ☐

 c. a firefighter ☐

 d. a baseball player ☐

 e. a chef ☐

 f. a pilot ☐

 g. a musician ☐

 h. a journalist ☐

 i. an artist ☐

 j. an actor ☐

3 🔘 💬 **Listen. Then talk together.**

1.  artist

2. pilot

3.  chef

4.  teachers

4 Read and say.

Explore Grammar

What	do	you	want to be?	I	want	to be	an actor.
	does	he she		He She	wants		

Why	do	you	want to be an actor?	Because	I	want	to be rich and famous.
	does	he she			he she	wants	

5 Listen and write.

1.
What? <u>He wants to be an artist.</u>

Why? <u>Because</u> _____

_____

_____

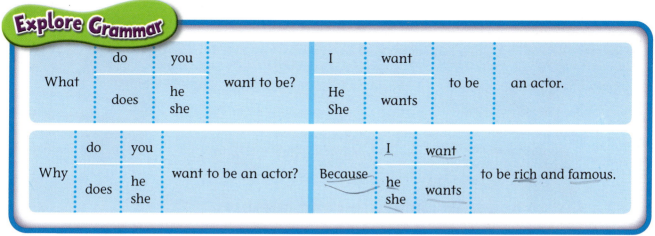

2.
What? _____

_____

Why? _____

_____

_____

3.
What? _____

_____

_____

Why? _____

_____

_____

4.
What? _____

_____

_____

Why? _____

_____

_____

6 Ask and answer.

What does he want to be?

Why does he want to be an artist?

He wants to be an artist.

Because he's good at painting.

7 🔘 **Listen and say.**

What do you want to be?

What do journalists do?

I want to be a journalist.

They write for newspapers.

8 🔘 **Listen and say. Then listen and number.**

a.   b.   c.   d.   e.

f.   g.   h.   i.   j.

◯ put out fires

◯ fly airplanes

◯ help sick people get better

◯ play baseball

◯ make music

◯ make great food

◯ make art

◯ help students learn

◯ write for newspapers

◯ act in movies

9 🎨 **Play.**

Do you work in a hospital?

Do you help people learn?

Are you a teacher?

No, I don't.

Yes, I do.

Yes, I am!

10 💿 📖 **Listen. Then read and write. Role-play.**

① Mulan, Ling, and Chien-Po are training to be soldiers.

You're the worst soldiers I've ever seen!

② After training, they have dinner.

I'm so tired.

I've never worked this hard before.

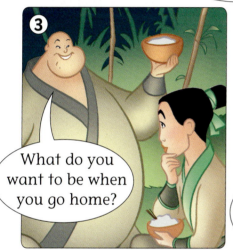

③ What do you want to be when you go home?

④ Mulan thinks about the question.

I think I want to be a teacher.

⑤ Like Captain Li?

No! Not like Captain Li!

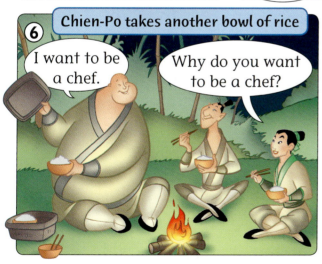

⑥ Chien-Po takes another bowl of rice

I want to be a chef.

Why do you want to be a chef?

⑦ Because I'm always hungry and I love food!

1. What does Mulan want to be? _____

2. Why does Chien-Po want to be a chef? _____

_____

Story **47**

Special Jobs

Some people have very special jobs! Here are two people with really special and exciting jobs!

An Astronaut

This is an astronaut. Astronauts work in space. Their job is to fly a space shuttle. They fly space shuttles just like a pilot. Sometimes they can go outside the space shuttle and walk in space. The Earth looks so beautiful from space! Do you want to be an astronaut?

A Clown Doctor

This is a clown doctor. Clown doctors work in hospitals. Their job is to make children happy. When children go to the hospital they're sad because they're sick. Clown doctors tell jokes to help them feel better. Do you want to be a clown doctor?

12 💬 **Ask and answer.**

1. Where do astronauts work?
2. What looks so beautiful from space?
3. Why are children sad when they're in the hospital?
4. How do clown doctors make children happy?

New Words

special, go outside, looks beautiful, space shuttle, space, children, sick, tell jokes, feel better

13 **Talk about dream jobs.**

What's your dream job? Why?

14 **Write and draw your dream job!**

I'm a _____

I work _____

_____

_____

_____

_____

_____

_____

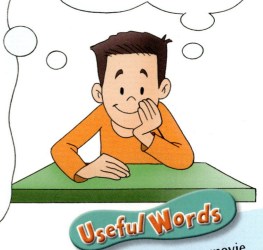

Useful Words

banker, lawyer, movie director, senator, train conductor, TV reporter

15 **Tell the class.**

Unit Wrap-up

16 **Listen and check. Then sing.** (See page 80.)

Listen and read.

When Two Worlds Meet

Pocahontas lived in the country. Her people didn't live in houses. They lived in wigwams. Her father was Powhatan.

Powhatan wanted Pocahontas to be Kocoum's wife. Kocoum was a very strong and brave man.

Pocahontas went to Grandmother Willow. "What should I do?" she asked. "You'll need to listen with your heart," said Grandmother Willow.

One day, Pocahontas saw a man next to a waterfall. She wanted to know who he was. She went down to the waterfall.

His name was John Smith. He was from England, but she didn't talk to him because she didn't understand English.

Then she remembered the words of Grandmother Willow… she listened with her heart … "Pocahontas," she said to him. "My name's Pocahontas."

  Ask and answer. Then write.

1. Who's Powhatan? _____

   _____

2. What did Grandmother Willow say to Pocahontas? _____

   _____

3. Why didn't Pocahontas talk to John Smith? _____

   _____

50

3 Play.

START!

1 What do you want to be when you're older?

2 Have you ever been to Peru?

3 What do teachers do?

4 Miss a turn!

5 Is Mushu grumpy?

6 Do you want to be a chef?

7 Do you like fries?

8 Go back 2 spaces.

9 What would you like for breakfast tomorrow?

10 What will you do first?

11 Go forward 2 spaces.

12 Are you good at cooking?

13 You're going to Peru. What will you need?

14 What's your father's name?

15 What classes do you have on Fridays?

16 Miss a turn!

17 Name 3 animals.

18 Do you live in the city or the country?

19 Why does your friend want to be an artist?

20 Do you have any brothers or sisters?

FINISH!

51

7 What Was He Doing?

1 Listen and say.

I saw David downtown yesterday.

He was reading a magazine.

No. I was on the bus at the time!

Really? What was he doing?

Did you say hello?

2 Listen and say. Then listen and number.

watching a movie

getting a haircut

renting a DVD

eating a pretzel

reading a magazine

shopping for clothes

3 Listen. Then talk together.

1. Mike / DVD   2. Coco / clothes   3. David / movie   4. Marina / haircut

4  **Read and say.**

Explore Grammar

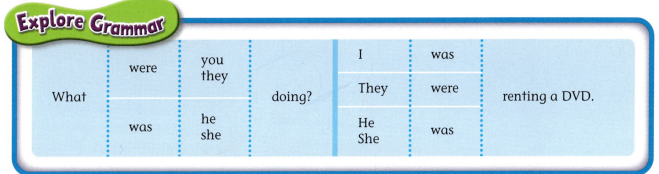

What	were	you they	doing?	I	was	renting a DVD.
	was	he she		They	were	
				He She	was	

5  **Listen and write.**

1. Andy _____

2. Emily and Pete _____

3. Martin and Amy _____

4. Anna _____

6  **Ask and answer.**

I saw Andy downtown yesterday.

He was shopping for clothes.

What was he doing?

7   **Ask 4 friends and write.**

What were you doing at 9 o'clock last night?

I was doing my homework.

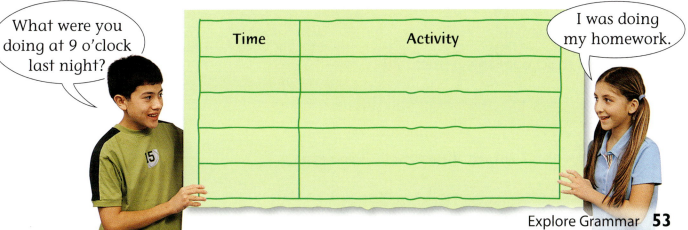

Time	Activity

8 🔘 **Listen and say.**

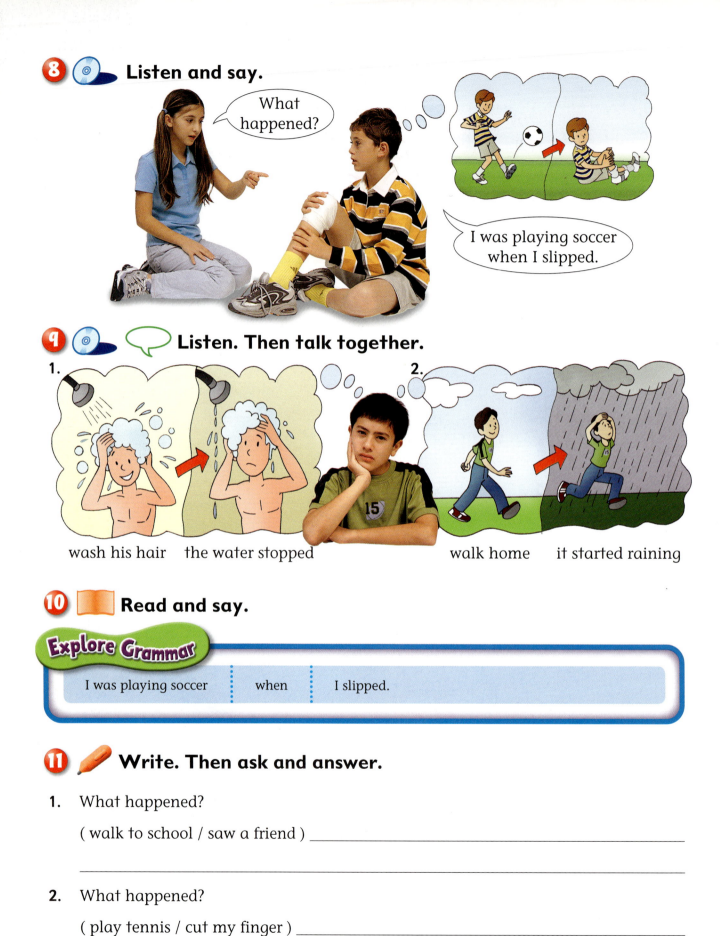

What happened?

I was playing soccer when I slipped.

9 🔘 💬 **Listen. Then talk together.**

1.

wash his hair   the water stopped

2.

walk home   it started raining

10 📖 **Read and say.**

Explore Grammar

| I was playing soccer | when | I slipped. |

11 🖊 **Write. Then ask and answer.**

1. What happened?

   (walk to school / saw a friend) _____

   _____

2. What happened?

   (play tennis / cut my finger) _____

   _____

12 🔘 📙 **Listen. Then read and write. Role-play.**

1 Aladdin visited Princess Jasmine.

I am Prince Ali!

Oh, great. Another prince!

2 Wait a minute. I've seen you before. In the market.

Really? What were you doing in the market?

3

I was ... uh ... shopping. A young man helped me. He looked like you.

Well, it wasn't me. I was relaxing in my big palace.

4 Jasmine walked away from Aladdin.

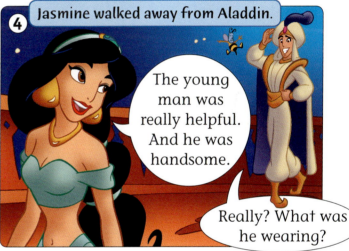

The young man was really helpful. And he was handsome.

Really? What was he wearing?

5 Jasmine turned around.

Well, he wasn't wearing a silly prince's hat!

Genie, help!

6 Is this better?

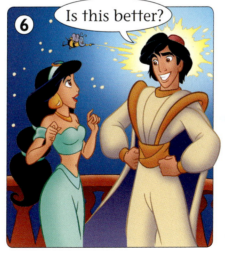

7 That's better!

1. What was Jasmine doing in the market? _____

2. Was the young man helpful and handsome? _____

Story **55**

13  **Listen and read.**

That's Embarrassing!

Sometimes we have some very embarrassing moments. Here are two embarrassing stories:

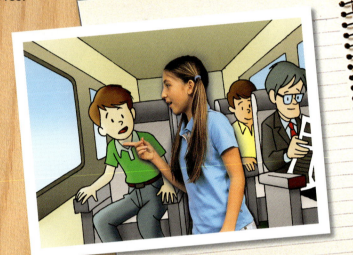

Oh, No!

I was on the train when I had an embarrassing moment. I was riding the train when I met a friend. We sat together and talked a long time about school and sports. We were talking when I saw that I missed my station! I was really embarrassed!

Be Quiet!

I was in the movie theater when I had an embarrassing moment. I was watching the movie with my friend when my cell phone rang! It was really loud! Everyone in the movie theater looked at me with angry faces. I was really embarrassed!

14 **Ask and answer.**

1. Who did Marina meet on the train?
2. Why didn't Marina get off the train at her station?
3. What was David doing when his cell phone rang?
4. Were the people in the movie theater happy?

New Words

embarrassing moment, cell phone, rang, missed my station

15 🗨 **Talk about embarrassing moments.**

Have you ever had an embarrassing moment? What happened?

16 ✏ **Write about your embarrassing moment.**

Useful Words

cooking, drinking, playing baseball, riding a bike, skateboarding, talking to a friend, watching TV

_____
_____
_____
_____
_____
_____
_____
_____

17 🗨 **Tell the class.**

Unit Wrap-up

18 💿 **Listen and number in order. Sing.** (See page 80.)

a.

slipped and fell down ☐

b.

cell phone rang ☐

c.

saw the rain ☐

8 Party Time

1 🔵 **Listen and say.**

> Have you made the corn dogs yet?

> I've bought the donuts, but I haven't bought the peanuts yet!

> Yes, I have. Have you bought the donuts?

> Hurry up! Our friends will be here soon.

2 🔵 **Listen and say. Then listen and write ✓ = Yes or ✗ = No.**

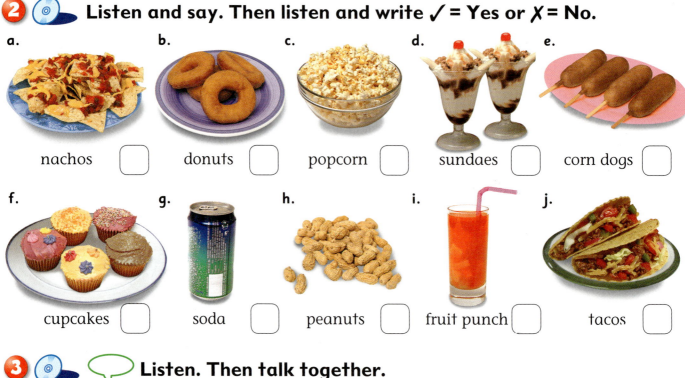

a. nachos ☐

b. donuts ☐

c. popcorn ☐

d. sundaes ☐

e. corn dogs ☐

f. cupcakes ☐

g. soda ☐

h. peanuts ☐

i. fruit punch ☐

j. tacos ☐

3 🔵 💬 **Listen. Then talk together.**

1. ✗

2. ✓

3. ✗

4. ✓

4  **Read and say.**

Have	you they	bought the corn dogs made the cake	yet?	Yes,	I they	have.	No,	I they	haven't.
Has	he she				he she	has.		he she	hasn't.

5  **Write.**

1.

Has he bought the nachos yet?
Yes, he has.

2.

_____
_____
_____

3.

_____
_____
_____

6 **Choose A or B. Then ask and answer.**

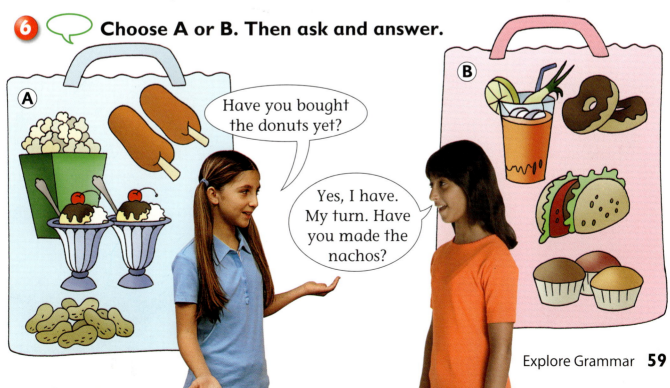

Have you bought the donuts yet?

Yes, I have. My turn. Have you made the nachos?

7 Listen and say.

Have you made the cake?

I've made the cake, but I haven't made the popcorn yet.

8 Listen and ✓ or ✗.

1. ✓ ✗

2. ☐ ☐

3. ☐ ☐

4. ☐ ☐

9 Check 5 items. Then ask and answer.

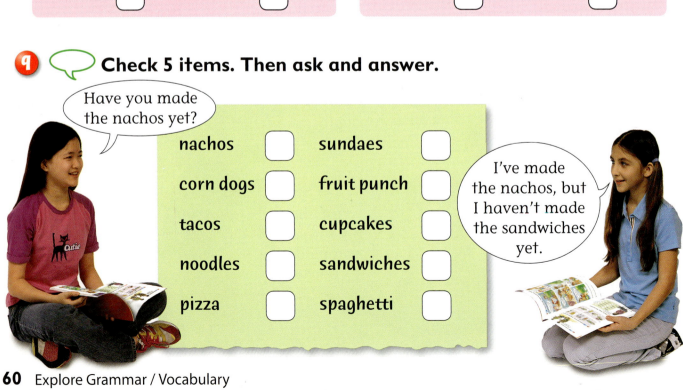

Have you made the nachos yet?

I've made the nachos, but I haven't made the sandwiches yet.

nachos ☐	sundaes ☐
corn dogs ☐	fruit punch ☐
tacos ☐	cupcakes ☐
noodles ☐	sandwiches ☐
pizza ☐	spaghetti ☐

10 🔘 Listen. Then read and write. Role-play.

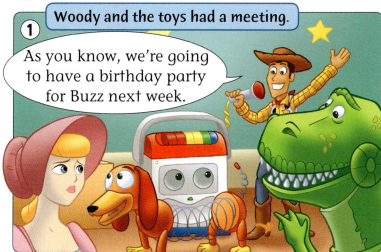

1. Why are they going to have a party? _____

_____

2. Has Rex made the banner? _____

Party Snacks

Children love going to parties, especially when there's a lot of food! Here are two party snacks you can make.

Ice Cream Sandwiches

The ingredients are simple for this snack. You only need two cookies and some ice cream. It's so easy. First, get some ice cream. Then, put the ice cream between the two cookies. That's it! Try them in the summer.

Popcorn Ball

You need brown sugar, butter, corn syrup, and popcorn. First, melt the sugar, butter, and syrup in a pan. Let it cool for 30 seconds. Then, add the popcorn and mix everything. Finally, use your hands to make a ball of popcorn. It's delicious!

12 💬 **Ask and answer.**

1. Why do children like parties?
2. When is the best season to eat ice cream sandwiches?
3. Which snack has the most ingredients?
4. Which snack is the easiest to make?

New Words

ingredients, simple, snack, sugar, butter, corn syrup, melt, cool, seconds, mix, finally, delicious

13  **Talk about party snacks.**

What party snacks are popular in your country?

14 **Write about a party snack.**

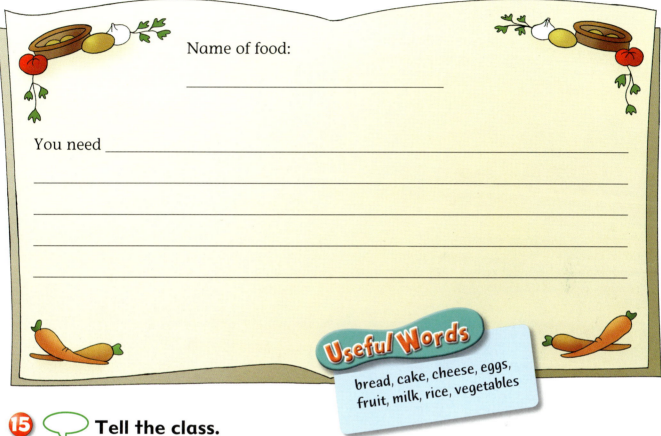

Name of food:

_____

You need _____

_____

_____

_____

_____

Useful Words

bread, cake, cheese, eggs, fruit, milk, rice, vegetables

15  **Tell the class.**

Unit Wrap-up

16 **Listen and write. Chant.** (See page 80.)

Let's Have a Party!

Have you called _____?

_____ cake?

Have _____ bought the _____?

Make sure _____!

1 **Listen and read.**

Meeting a Princess

Aladdin and Abu were walking down a street in the market when Aladdin saw a beautiful young woman. She was giving an apple to a boy.

"Have you paid for that apple yet?" a big man asked. The woman was scared. "I'm sorry. I don't have any money," she answered.

The man was angry, but Aladdin stepped between them. "I'm sorry," said Aladdin. "She's my crazy sister. Here's your apple."

They were walking away when Abu dropped some apples on the floor. "Stop!" shouted the big man, but they ran very fast.

Aladdin took the young woman to his home. They were looking at the palace when the king's soldiers saw them.

"Let him go!" the woman said. "I'm Princess Jasmine!" Everyone was surprised, but Aladdin was the most surprised! She was a princess!

2 **Ask and answer. Then write.**

1. What were Aladdin and Abu doing when they saw the young woman?

   _____

2. What were Aladdin and the young woman doing when the soldiers saw them?

   _____

3. Why were the soldiers and Aladdin surprised?

   _____

3  Play.

START

1 Would you like to be an astronaut?

2 How many toys are there on this page?

3 Miss a turn!

8 Who is the shortest? Slinky Dog, Rex, or Bullseye?

7 Go back 2 spaces.

6 How many toys do you have?

5 Name 3 jobs.

4 What toys do you have in your room?

9 Is Rex a dinosaur?

10 What do you do on weekends?

11 Miss a turn!

12 What were you doing at 6 o'clock yesterday?

17 Who is taller? You or your best friend?

16 Have you made the cake?

15 I have a cough. What should I do?

14 Go forward 2 spaces.

13 What were you wearing yesterday?

18 What time do you get up?

19 Have you ever been to a birthday party?

20 What's your favorite toy?

FINISH

1 Complete the puzzle with a partner. Student A and Student B use the information on page 67. Take turns saying clues and writing words.

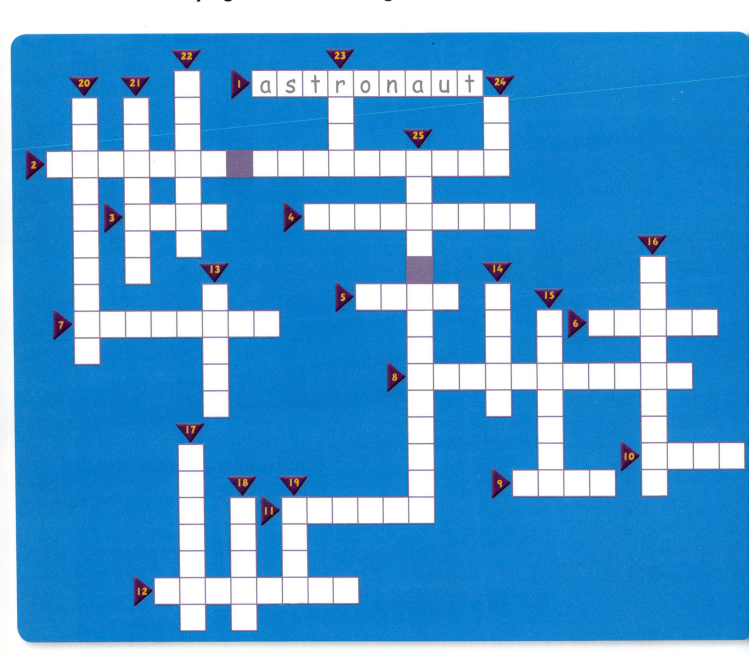

1. a s t r o n a u t

Student A

Across

1. a person who travels in a spaceship in space

2. The piano is a _____.

3. a person who cooks good food in restaurants

4. a drink with milk and ice cream, usually vanilla or chocolate

5. the past tense and participle of *make*

6. And _____ you like something to drink?

Down ▼

13. a celebration with people, food, and sometimes presents

14. made from potatoes, these are served with hamburgers

15. I'm hurt. I _____ and fell down.

16. things you buy to remember a vacation or trip

17. I was _____ the car when it began to rain.

18. Have you _____ dinner yet?

19. *good*, *better*, _____

Student B

Across

7. you carry your clothes in this when you travel

8. a person trained to put out fires

9. Have you ever _____ to Monterrey?

10. Rock musicians are _____ and famous.

11. Have you _____ food for the party?

12. The Wright brothers _____ the first airplane.

Down ▼

20. a person who works for a newspaper or with TV news

21. My hair's too long. I need a _____.

22. cheap, _____, cheapest

23. Let's _____ a DVD and watch it tonight.

24. Have you made your bed _____?

25. For me, math is the _____ subject at school.

Food Around the World

1   **Read and check.**

	True	False
1. People eat a lot of meat in South America.	☐	☐
2. In Italy, people don't eat much pasta.	☐	☐
3. In North America, people eat a lot of hot spices.	☐	☐
4. The Japanese eat a lot of fish and rice.	☐	☐
5. People eat a lot of meat and fish in Australia.	☐	☐

2 **Complete the sentences.**

The Japanese diet is a healthful way to eat.
The Japanese eat a lot of _____,
_____, and _____.
They cook their food for a _____ ___.
time so that the flavor and _____
aren't lost.

3   Write.

1. What is a very popular outdoor activity in Australia?

   _____

2. What equipment do people take with them to cook outdoors?

   _____

3. What kinds of foods are used for a barbecue?

   _____

4. What is food on a wooden or metal stick or skewer called?

   _____

5. What tropical fruits do Australians like eating?

   _____

4   What about you? Write.

In my country, we eat _____

_____

_____

In a typical day at home, I eat _____

_____

Is your typical diet healthful? Why or why not? _____

_____

Amazing Instruments

1 🖊 **Write the numbers.**

_____ number of keys in a piano _____ number of strings on a sitar

_____ number of keys in some organs _____ number of musicians in some orchestras

_____ number of meters in longest pipe _____ number of pipes in the biggest organ

2 🖊 **Write.**

1. What are some instruments in an orchestra?

_____

2. Which musical instrument is the biggest and loudest?

_____

3. Which is one of the biggest wind instruments?

_____

4. Where is the biggest organ in the world?

_____

5. What country do sitars come from?

_____

3 🖊 **What about you? Write.**

1. Which instruments do you like listening to?

_____

2. Can you play a musical instrument? Which one?

_____

3. What are two of your favorite bands?

_____

Balloons

1 **How does a balloon fly? Number the sentences in order.**

[ ] Up in the sky, the wind blows and pushes the balloon around.

[ ] The pilot lights the gas in the burner.

[ ] Without the burner, the air in the balloon gets cold.

[ ] The pilot and passengers get into the balloon basket.

[ ] The balloon falls slowly to the ground.

[ ] The pilot turns off the gas burner.

[ ] The burner's hot air fills the balloon and lifts it into the sky.

2 **Complete the sentences.**

The first balloon flew above Paris in _____.

Two _____, Jacques and Joseph

Montgolfier, invented the balloon. Their

balloon didn't fly very _____, but their

flight lasted for an _____. Today, we

think airplanes are more _____

than balloons, because pilots can control them

and they are much _____. But

many people still love balloons as a sport.

3 **Compare balloons and airplanes.**

Similarities	Differences

Wheels

  **Write.**

1. Where did wheels first appear? How long ago?

   _____

2. Were the first wheels solid, or did they have holes in them?

   _____

3. Why were holes in wheels useful?

   _____

4. Who invented the modern wheel? When?

   _____

5. How was a boy on a tricycle part of the invention of the modern wheel?

   _____

2 **Write.**

1. What are ten things that use some kind of wheel?

   _____

   _____

   _____

2. What are the differences among a unicycle, a bicycle, and a tricycle?

   _____

   _____

   _____

3. Imagine you have a chance to ride a unicycle, ride in an old-fashioned balloon, or ride in an old-fashioned airplane like the Wright brothers' plane. Which one do you want to try? Why?

   _____

   _____

Egyptian Games

1 ✏️ **Complete the sentences.**

1. The pyramids are the most famous Egyptian _____.

2. We can learn about daily life in ancient Egypt through smaller things, such as toys and musical _____.

3. In a museum, you can see a toy _____ that still opens and closes its mouth.

4. An ancient game called _____. was very popular with Egyptians.

5. People played the game on a special _____.

6. One example of a Senet table was in the royal _____ of the Egyptian ruler, King Tutankhamun.

2 ✏️ **What about you? Write.**

Toys I Like	Board Games I Like

3 **Number your favorites in order.**

1 = most favorite   6 = least favorite

◯ video games

◯ board games

◯ puzzles

◯ drawing and painting

◯ playing an instrument

◯ dolls or action figures

Going Places

 1 🖊 **Write complete sentences.**

1. What are four typical ways people travel in cities?

_____

2. What are some transportation problems in cities?

_____

3. What are some ways of traveling that don't cause these problems?

_____

4. Where can you see rickshaws as a form of transportation?

_____

5. Do people travel in sedan chairs today? Why or why not?

_____

6. Where can you probably see businessmen on rollerblades?

_____

2 **Check the chart.**

City Transportation						
	causes pollution	causes noise	expensive	fast	good exercise	not used today
bicycle						
bus						
rickshaw						
rollerblades						
sedan chair						
skateboard						
subway						
taxi						

 3 **Write.**

What form of transportation do you usually use? Why?

_____

_____

Emergency Vet

1 Complete the sentences.

Doctors who work with animals are called _____. Sarah Green is an emergency vet. Her specialty is birds, particularly big birds such as _____ and _____. When these birds get lost or hurt, Sarah _____ them. If they are lost, she takes them to a _____, because they need _____. If they are hurt, she looks after them until they are _____. Like other vets, Sarah also works with sick dogs and _____, and other animals too.

2 Read and check.

	True	False
1. Swans are very clever animals.	☐	☐
2. Swans can't take off from the ground.	☐	☐
3. Swans can always find the way back to water.	☐	☐
4. Swans are strong birds.	☐	☐
5. Swans and geese can't bite.	☐	☐

3 Read and answer.

Vets work with sick animals. Other people work with animals too. For example, there are animal trainers who work with circus animals, such as lions and elephants. There are people who train dogs to act correctly in peoples' homes. There are biologists who study wild animals, like apes or monkeys, in their natural habitats. There are animal wranglers who teach animals to act in movies. And there are dog walkers who exercise the animals of busy people who don't have time, and cat sitters who stay with the cats while their owners are traveling.

1. Do you like animals?

_____

2. When you are older, do you want to do one of these jobs? Why or why not?

_____

Soccer

  **Write.**

1. What is the world's most popular sport?

   _____

2. Is soccer an old game or a modern game?

   _____

3. When did modern rules for soccer appear?

   _____

4. When and where was the first World Cup?

   _____

5. What are some countries with women's soccer teams?

   _____

6. When was the first women's World Cup?

   _____

 Compare soccer and American football.

	Soccer	Football
ball		
uniform		
helmets		
rules		
players		

  What about you? Write.

1. Do you like to watch soccer? Play soccer? Why or why not?

   _____

2. Who's your favorite soccer team? Why?

   _____

3. Are women good soccer players? Why or why not?

   _____

A Cool Treat

1   **Write.**

1. Where did the idea for ice cream come from?

_____

2. What did the Emperor Nero mix with fruits and honey to make a kind of ice cream?

_____

_____

3. Where do people make ice cream in metal bowls?

_____

4. Does ice cream take a short time to make?

_____

5. Is ice cream good for you? How do you know?

_____

2 Circle things we use to make and eat ice cream.

bowl   China   chocolate   cream   cone   dish   eggs   fork   fruit   honey
ice   juice   pizza   protein   rice   salt   spoon   sugar   treat   vanilla   water

3   **Write.**

1. What's your favorite ice cream?

_____

2. When do you eat ice cream—on special days or any day?

_____

3. What do you like to eat with your ice cream?

_____

Songs and Chants

 The *English Adventure* Theme Song

We're going on an English Adventure.
We're going to have lots of fun.
We're going on an English Adventure.
You, me, and everyone!
You, me, and everyone!

Rub, rub, rub on Aladdin's lamp,
We'll ask Genie for a wish.
We'll meet old friends like Mickey Mouse,
And make new ones like Lilo and Stitch.

We're going on an English Adventure.
We're going to have lots of fun.
We're going on an English Adventure.
You, me, and everyone!
You, me, and everyone!

Castles and jungles and islands in the
 sun,
New worlds wait for you and me.
Monsters and mermaids and beasts and
 bugs,
And pirates in the deep, blue sea.

We're going on an English Adventure.
We're going to have lots of fun.
We're going on an English Adventure.
You, me, and everyone!
You, me, and everyone!

Clap, clap, clap, come on girls and boys!
Stamp, stamp, stamp, come on and make
 some noise!
Rub your head and wiggle your nose,
Pat your knees and touch your toes!

We're going on an English Adventure.
We're going to have lots of fun.
We're going on an English Adventure.
You, me, and everyone!
You, me, and everyone!
You, me, and everyone!

Hello! Unit

 Chant (page 8)

I can run one hundred meters.
I can run one thousand meters.
We can run. We can run.
Run together. Let's have fun!

[repeat all]

Unit 1

 Chant (page 15)

What would you like?
I'd like a hot dog.
A hot dog and a milkshake.
A hot dog and a milkshake?
Yes. A hot dog and a milkshake.

How about you?

What would you like?
I'd like fried chicken.
Fried chicken and salad.
Fried chicken and salad?
Yes. Fried chicken and salad.

[repeat all]

Unit 2

 Song (page 21)

Who can play the tambourine?
Who can play it?
They can.
Can they play the guitar too?
Can they play it?
They can.

Keyboards, trumpets, tambourines too.
They're much better than me or you.
Keyboards, trumpets, tambourines too.
They're much better than me or you.

Can they play the keyboard too?
Can they play it?
They can.
Can they play the trumpet too?
Can they play it?
They can.

Keyboards, trumpets, tambourines too.
They're much better than me or you.
Keyboards, trumpets, tambourines too.
They're much better than me or you.

They're much better than me or you!

Unit 3

 ## Song (page 29)

What did you do last Saturday?
I studied history.
Potato chips were invented
In 1853.

That was a very long time ago
In a different century.
It's a very very old invention.
It's older than you and me.

What did you do this afternoon?
I studied history.
The hot-air balloon was invented
In 1783.

That was a very long time ago
In a different century.
It's a very very old invention.
It's older than you and me.

Unit 4

 ## Song (page 35)

Milkshake, soda, lemonade, tea.
I've had all these drinks before.
Pizza, steak, salad, and fries.
I've eaten all these foods and more.

But I haven't been to France.
I haven't been to Rome.
When can I travel around the world?
I don't want to stay home.

Bowling, surfing, and basketball.
I've watched all these sports before.
Tennis, soccer, and baseball too.
I've played all these sports and more.

But I haven't been to France.
I haven't been to Rome.
When can I travel around the world?
I don't want to stay home.

I don't want to stay home!

Unit 5

 ## Song (page 43)

We're going away! We're going away!
To a country overseas!
Where will you go?
What will you do?
We all want to know.
Where will you go?
What will you do?

We'll go to Italy.
We'll make a lot of new friends.
We'll study and practice our Italian.
And we'll have fun on the weekends.

We're going away! We're going away!
To a country overseas!
Where will you go?
What will you do?
We all want to know.
Where will you go?
What will you do?

We'll go to Hong Kong tomorrow.
We'll need to take some money.
We won't need to take a warm jacket.
The weather will be very sunny!

We're going away! We're going away!
To a country overseas!
Where will you go?
What will you do?
We all want to know.
Where will you go?
What will you do?

Unit 6

 ### Song (page 49)

I want to be a chef
And make lots of good food.
I want to be a pilot
And fly around the world.

I want to be a teacher
And teach English all day.
I want to be an artist
And paint pictures my way!

[repeat all]

Unit 7

 ### Song (page 57)

It was a bad day for us all yesterday.
The weather was cold and the sky was
    so gray.

I was playing baseball
    when I slipped and fell down.
I cut my right knee
    and I made a loud sound.

It was a bad day for us all yesterday.
The weather was cold and the sky was
    so gray.

I was walking outside
    when I saw the rain.
I had no umbrella
    and I missed the train.

It was a bad day for us all yesterday.
The weather was cold and the sky was
    so gray.

I was watching a show
    when my cell phone rang.
Someone looked at me.
An angry old man!

It was a bad day for us all yesterday.
The weather was cold and the sky was
    so gray.

Unit 8

 ### Chant (page 63)

Party! Party!
Lets celebrate today!
Party! Party!
Lets celebrate today!

Have you called your friends?
Have you made the cake?
Have you bought the donuts?
Make sure you're not late!

[repeat all]

_____

_____

_____

_____

_____

_____

_____

_____

_____

_____

_____

_____

_____

_____

_____

_____

_____

_____

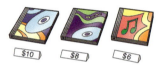

_____

_____

_____

_____

$$39 \times 52 =$$
$$206 \div 2.4 =$$
$$0.8 \times 9 \div 12 =$$

1839

$$30 \times 3 =$$
$$10 - 2 =$$
$$1 + 1 =$$

1,500

_____

500

_____

_____

_____

_____

_____

_____

_____

_____

_____

_____

_____

_____

_____

_____

_____

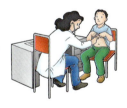

_____

_____

_____

_____

_____

_____

_____

_____

_____

_____

_____

_____

_____

_____

_____

_____

_____

_____

1915

_____

1998

100,000

1,000,000

1,000

1004

_____

_____

_____

_____

_____

_____

_____

_____

_____

_____

_____

_____

1700

10,000

2006

Grammar Review

Unit 1 At the Restaurant

Waiter: What **would** you **like**?
Mom: **I'd like** chicken salad and some tea, please.
Waiter: And the kids?
Mom: **They'd like** hot dogs with fries.
Waiter: **Would** they **like** a drink with that?
Kids: **We'd like** lemonade, please.

Waiter: Here's your bill. How was your meal?
Mom: Good, thanks. **How much is it**?
Waiter: **It's** $12.45.
Mom: Here you are. And a tip.
Waiter: Thanks.

Unit 2 They're the Best!

Ana: I like that music. Who **are** you **listening to**?
Pat: Super Salsa. It's their new CD.
Ana: Wow. They're even **better than** the Rhythm Rockers.
Pat: Yeah. They're **the best**!

Ken: Look! All these CDs are on sale.
Tim: And here's a CD by Canela. It isn't **expensive**.
Ken: This Enrique Iglesias CD is **more expensive than** the Canela CD.
Tim: Well, I'm getting this CD by Shakira. It's **the most expensive**, but I really like her music.

Mom: Please turn down that music. It's too **loud**.
Sue: What? Speak **louder**.
Mom: PLEASE TURN DOWN THE MUSIC!
Sue: Wow, Mom. You have **the loudest** voice in the house!

Unit 3 Inventions

Ana: When **were** jeans **invented**?
Eva: They **were invented** in 1850 by Levi Strauss.

Jan: What was the name of the Wright brothers' plane?
Ted: It **was called** the Kitty Hawk.
Jan: When did they build their plane?
Ted: They built it in 1903.

Unit 4 Experiences

Ken: **Have** you ever **been** to Colombia?
Eva: No, I **haven't**. **Have** you?
Ken: Yes, I **have**.
Eva: When did you go?
Ken: I went last year, to Cartegena. It was great.

Pat: **Has** your brother ever **practiced** judo?
Tom: No, he **hasn't**. But he practices tae-kwon-do.
Pat: I want to learn that!

Unit 5 See the World

Ted: Look! The plane is landing. We're finally here!

Jim: This is so exciting. I'm looking forward to meeting out host family.

Ted: Me too. It **will be** fun living with them for a whole month!

Jim: What **will** you **do** first?

Ted: I**'ll call** my family and **tell** them everything is OK. And you?

Jim: I **won't call**. I**'ll send** an e-mail home. It's cheaper!

Dad: What **will** Linda **need** for her camping trip?

Mom: She**'ll need** some new hiking boots.

Dad: **Will** she **need** a new jacket?

Mom: No, she **won't**. Her old jacket is fine.

Unit 6 My Dream Job

Ana: What do you **want to be** when you're older?

Bill: I **want to be** a soccer player.

Ana: Really? **Why** do you want to be a soccer player?

Bill: **Because** I love sports, and I'm good at playing soccer.

Lou: What does your brother **want to be**?

Art: He **wants to be** a journalist.

Lou: What **do** journalists **do**?

Art: They **write** for newspapers.

Unit 7 What Was He Doing?

Liz: I **saw** our teacher downtown on Saturday.

Ken: What **was** she **doing**?

Liz: She **was looking at** books in the bookstore.

Ken: **Did** you **say** hello?

Liz: No, I **didn't**. I see her five days every week!

Bob: What **were** your parents **doing** at the mall?

Tom: I don't know. Maybe they **were buying** my birthday present!

Pat: Look at your clothes! They're completely wet!

Bill: I know. I **was walking** home **when** it **started** to rain.

Unit 8 Party Time

Jon: **Have** you **made** Ana's birthday cake yet?

Sue: No, I **haven't**. Carmen is going to help me.
Have you **bought** the balloons yet?

Jon: Yes, I **have**.

Kim: **Have** your parents **bought** the plane tickets yet?

Art: Yes, they **have**. But we **haven't packed** our suitcases yet.

Kim: Well, you have two more days.

Lou: **Has** Sonia **finished** her homework yet?

Pat: Yes, she **has**. Why?

Lou: I need her help with math!

Common Irregular Verbs

Base Form	Simple Past	Past Participle
be: am/is/are	was/were	been
break	broke	broken
bring	brought	brought
build	built	built
buy	bought	bought
come	came	come
cost	cost	cost
cut	cut	cut
do	did	done
draw	drew	drawn
drink	drank	drunk
eat	ate	eaten
fall	fell	fallen
feel	felt	felt
find	found	found
fly	flew	flown
get	got	gotten
give	gave	given
go	went	gone
have: have/has	had	had
hide	hid	hidden
know	knew	known
make	made	made
meet	met	met
pay	paid	paid
read	read	read
ride	rode	ridden
ring	rang	rung
run	ran	run
say	said	said
see	saw	seen
send	sent	sent
sing	sang	sung
swim	swam	swum
take	took	taken
tell	told	told
think	thought	thought
throw	threw	thrown
wear	wore	worn
write	wrote	written

Word List